GL
THE GOSPELS

THE KINGDOM OF GOD
The Essential Message of Jesus

Frank J. Matera

Little Rock
Scripture Study

A ministry of the Diocese of Little Rock
in partnership with Liturgical Press

Nihil obstat: Jerome Kodell, OSB, *Censor Librorum.*
Imprimatur: ✛ Anthony B. Taylor, Bishop of Little Rock, March 20, 2019.

Cover design by Ann Blattner. Cover photo: Getty Images. Used with permission.

Photos/illustrations: Pages 8, 10, 12, 16, 20, 24, 26, 28, 29, 33, 38, 40, Getty Images. Used with permission.

ISBN: 978-0-8146-6450-6 (print); 978-0-8146-6475-9 (e-book)

Contents

Introduction

Alive in the Word brings you resources to deepen your understanding of Scripture, offer meaning for your life today, and help you to pray and act in response to God's word.

Use any volume of **Alive in the Word** in the way best suited to you.

- **For individual learning and reflection,** consider this an invitation to prayerfully journal in response to the questions you find along the way. And be prepared to move from head to heart and then to action.

- **For group learning and reflection,** arrange for three sessions where you will use the material provided as the basis for faith sharing and prayer. You may ask group members to read each chapter in advance and come prepared with questions answered. In this kind of session, plan to be together for about an hour. Or, if your group prefers, read and respond to the questions together without advance preparation. With this approach, it's helpful to plan on spending more time for each group session in order to adequately work through each of the chapters.

- **For a parish-wide event or use within a larger group,** provide each person with a copy of this volume, and allow time during the event for quiet reading, group discussion and prayer, and then a final commitment by each person to some simple action in response to what he or she learned.

This volume on the topic of the kingdom of God is one of several volumes that explore **Gleanings from the Gospels.** The richness of the gospel tradition stands at the heart of Christian teaching and reveals to us in a unique way the truth of God's extravagant love. Each evangelist paints a portrait of Jesus that is unique in some respects and yet, taken together, they reveal a whole that is quite remarkable. The images and teachings found through the four gospels provide every generation with the tools that form disciples. By reflecting on the threads that run through the gospel accounts, we become part of the tapestry that is Christianity.

Prologue

The central message that Jesus proclaimed was the appearance of the kingdom of God in his ministry. In the Gospel according to Mark, Jesus begins his ministry by saying, "This is the time of fulfillment. The kingdom of God is at hand. Repent, and believe in the gospel" (Mark 1:15). Thereafter, everything he says and everything he does proclaims the kingdom of God. Jesus' mighty deeds, whereby he cures the sick and drives out demons, show that God's rule is invading human history. Similarly, his teaching deals with the appearance of God's kingdom.

But what did Jesus mean by the kingdom of God? What was he waiting and hoping for? A helpful way to understand what Jesus meant is to read Psalms 93 and 95–99, which proclaim that God is Israel's king. These and other psalms celebrate God's rule or kingship over history and creation. For example, "The LORD is king. / The world will surely stand fast, never to be shaken. / He rules the people with fairness" (Ps 96:10). As Creator, God rules over creation; and as the Savior of Israel, God rules over human history.

When Jesus proclaims that the kingdom of God is making its appearance in his ministry, he is saying that God is reclaiming his rule over creation that has rebelled against God's rule. The salvation that the kingdom of God brings, then, is cosmic in scope, for in Jesus' ministry God is restoring the order of creation and history.

As we explore three gospel passages about the kingdom of God, we will reflect on the presence of the kingdom, the mystery of the kingdom, and the universal scope of the kingdom. We will also reflect on how we experience the saving reality of the kingdom of God in our own lives.

The Presence of the Kingdom of God

Begin by asking God to assist you in your prayer and study. Then read Matthew 12:22-30, which describes an event that allows Jesus to proclaim the clear choice for God's kingdom.

Matthew 12:22-30

²²Then they brought to him a demoniac who was blind and mute. He cured the mute person so that he could speak and see. ²³All the crowd was astounded, and said, "Could this perhaps be the Son of David?" ²⁴But when the Pharisees heard this, they said, "This man drives out demons only by the power of Beelzebul, the prince of demons." ²⁵But he knew what they were thinking and said to them, "Every kingdom divided against itself will be laid waste, and no town or house divided against itself will stand. ²⁶And if Satan drives out

Satan, he is divided against himself; how, then, will his kingdom stand? ²⁷And if I drive out demons by Beelzebul, by whom do your own people drive them out? Therefore they will be your judges. ²⁸But if it is by the Spirit of God that I drive out demons, then the kingdom of God has come upon you. ²⁹How can anyone enter a strong man's house and steal his property, unless he first ties up the strong man? Then he can plunder his house. ³⁰Whoever is not with me is against me, and whoever does not gather with me scatters."

Following a few moments of quiet reflection on Matthew 12:22-30, review the background information provided in "Setting the Scene." This context will help to situate the scene in the story line Matthew provides. Occasional questions in the margins are for group sharing or personal reflection or journaling.

Setting the Scene

The kingdom of God is both a present and a future reality. On the one hand, the kingdom has already made its appearance in the life and ministry of Jesus, as this passage will illustrate. It is not a far distant reality for which we are still waiting and hoping; it is something that we can already experience here and now in the person of Jesus and in the community of believers. On the other hand, as our next passage will show, there is also a future dimension to the kingdom that will be revealed at the end of the ages. Thus, Christians live "between the times" in a creative

The commentary describes the "creative tension" of the kingdom of God as already present but not yet fully realized. How do you experience this "creative tension" in your own life?

tension. The kingdom has *already* made its initial appearance in the person of Jesus Christ, but the fullness of the kingdom has *not yet* made its appearance. It is this tension between *already* and *not yet* that gives purpose and dynamism to our lives as we already experience something of the final salvation for which we wait and hope.

The passage we are considering belongs to a larger section of the Gospel of Matthew in which Jesus encounters growing opposition to his ministry (11:1–12:50). Faced with this opposition, Jesus describes his contemporaries as impossible to please because they accused John the Baptist of being an ascetic and him of being a glutton (11:16-19). He then warns the towns of Galilee where he performed most of his mighty deeds because they failed to repent (11:20-24). Next, the Pharisees accuse Jesus' disciples of violating the Sabbath (12:1-8), and they conspire to put him to death because he has healed on the Sabbath (12:9-14). As we come to our passage, there has already been clear opposition to Jesus and his ministry. As we shall see, neither the people nor their leaders have understood and embraced his message about the kingdom.

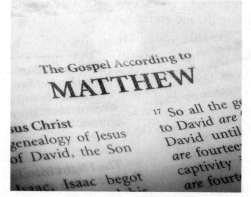

The passage from Matthew 12:22-30 will be considered a few verses at a time in the section below. Continue to use the questions in the margins either for group discussion or personal reflection.

Understanding the Scene Itself

²²**Then they brought to him a demoniac who was blind and mute. He cured the mute person so that he could speak and see.** ²³**All the crowd was astounded, and said, "Could this perhaps be the Son of David?"**

In the episode immediately preceding this passage, Matthew summarizes Jesus' ministry of healing Israel (12:15-16) and applies to him a passage from the prophet Isaiah that portrays Jesus as God's beloved and humble servant who brings justice to the nations (12:17-21; Isa 42:1-4). Jesus has healed so many that the people bring him a man who is blind and unable to speak because he is possessed by a demon. This man is us! He represents the human condition oppressed by the rule of Satan. Under this oppressive rule, humanity is blind to God's rule over history and creation; and because it is blind to God's rule, it is unable to praise and glorify with its lips the one God who rules over history and creation. We are blind and mute; we need to be healed and ushered into God's kingdom.

Matthew's description of the healing is brief and without adornment. He simply notes that Jesus cured the man so that he could speak and see. Although there is no mention of Jesus casting

Can you relate to the blind and mute man who was brought to Jesus to be healed? In what ways does blindness and muteness affect your own life as you wait for God's kingdom in its fullness?

As modern readers, we are not accustomed to language about "kingdoms" and "rule." How do you understand what it means to be "under God's rule" (like the man healed by Jesus)? How might we speak about this in more contemporary language?

out the demon, this is precisely what happens. The man can see and speak because he is no longer under the power of Satan; he has been brought into the kingdom of God and is now under God's rule.

The astounded crowd begins to understand the significance of what Jesus has done and asks if Jesus might be the Son of David, that is, the Messiah. David was the greatest of Israel's kings, and when his dynasty ended at the time of Israel's exile in Babylon (sixth century BC), God's people waited and hoped for a new David who would restore God's rule over their lives. Because of the power of this healing whereby Jesus overcomes the power of Satan, the crowd asks if he might be this long-awaited Son of David.

24But when the Pharisees heard this, they said, "This man drives out demons only by the power of Beelzebul, the prince of demons."

The Pharisees, however, are already plotting to put Jesus to death because they see him as a

lawbreaker who violates the Sabbath (12:14); they do not agree with what the crowd has said. The Pharisees acknowledge that Jesus has cast out a demon, but they interpret what has occurred in a perverse way: what Jesus has done is not the work of God but the work of Satan. Jesus, they say, has cast out this demon by the power of Beelzebul (another name for Satan). In their view, Jesus' ministry is a manifestation of the kingdom of evil rather than the kingdom of God. Their opposition to Jesus could not be stronger; they call evil what is good, and they identify God's agent with the "prince of demons."

In this story, the Pharisees do not recognize who Jesus truly is, and so they oppose him. In what ways do we fail to recognize Jesus and the presence of the kingdom of God? Why does this happen, and how can we learn to recognize him?

[25]But he knew what they were thinking and said to them, "Every kingdom divided against itself will be laid waste, and no town or house divided against itself will stand. [26]And if Satan drives out Satan, he is divided against himself; how, then, will his kingdom stand? [27]And if I drive out demons by Beelzebul, by whom do your own people drive them out? Therefore, they will be your judges. [28]But if it is by the Spirit of God that I drive out demons, then the kingdom of God has come upon you."

Matthew notes that even though the Pharisees did not criticize Jesus to his face, he "knew what they were thinking." They have opposed him from the beginning because they refuse to believe his central proclamation that the kingdom of God is making its appearance in his ministry. Their opposition, however, does not surprise Jesus. Those who refuse to believe that the kingdom of God is making its appearance in his ministry cannot understand the significance of his mighty deeds. Jesus is more than a miracle worker; he is God's Messiah who ushers in the kingdom by his powerful deeds of healing and casting out demons.

Jesus' practical argument that "no house divided against itself will stand" has implications for every community. What are some of the sources of division in your family, parish, or community? Describe some possible solutions for healing the divide.

Jesus' response to the Pharisees is threefold. First, he lays bare the foolishness of their charge against him. If what they are thinking about him is true, then Satan is working at cross-purposes with himself. He is destroying his own rule over humanity by freeing humanity from its bondage to evil. Satan is destroying his own kingdom, his own house. Why would Satan drive out Satan? Why would Satan free his subjects from his rule and dominion? If the power of Jesus is a manifestation of the power of Satan, then Satan's house is already crumbling. In a phrase made famous by Abraham Lincoln during the Civil War, "A house divided against itself cannot stand."

In verse 27, Jesus raises another objection against the Pharisees. He is not the only one who casts out demons. There were others in Israel who did the same. Exorcists were not uncommon in the ancient world, and the Pharisees would have readily acknowledged this. But if Jesus casts out demons by the power of Beelzebul, by what power do their own exorcists cast out demons: by the power of God or by the power of Satan? The answer is obvious: every exorcism is a manifestation of God's power, not the power of evil. Satan takes possession and enslaves people; God liberates and releases them from bondage.

"Exorcism" or "casting out demons" is not something we commonly experience or think about today. Do you believe in the existence of evil? Where do you see or experience it?

Verse 28 is the climax of Jesus' argument, and it reveals what is happening in his ministry. If Jesus casts out demons by the power of God's Spirit, *then the kingdom of God has come upon all who experience his ministry*. Jesus' exorcisms and healings are not just miracles. They are

> **Although sickness is not a result of sin, it is an indication that there is something awry, something that is not yet whole in God's good creation.**

mighty deeds that point to something—the kingdom of God. When Jesus cures the sick, he is pushing back the boundaries of Satan's rule. When he casts out demons, he is pushing back the boundaries of Satan's rule. Jesus is engaged in a cosmic battle between the kingdom of God and the power of evil. He is not merely restoring the sight and speech of a man; he is invading and destroying Satan's kingdom by pushing back its boundaries to make room for God's rule. This is why the kingdom of God is already present in Jesus' ministry.

Sickness has a profound meaning in our lives. It reminds us of our mortality; it makes us aware of our human weakness. Although sickness is not a result of sin, it is an indication that there is something awry, something that is not yet whole in God's good creation. This is why Jesus' ministry to the sick and our ministry to the sick are so important. Sickness is an indication that creation is still frustrated by the existence of evil. It is an indication of our profound need for God's grace and the fullness of God's kingdom.

Have you experienced a serious illness or the illness of a loved one? How did you understand this illness in the context of your faith?

"²⁹How can anyone enter a strong man's house and steal his property, unless he first ties up the strong man? Then he can plunder his house."

The second step in Jesus' explanation to the Pharisees about his ministry is a revelation of why he is able to expel demons: he is stronger than Satan. Jesus is the one who has already bound him and plundered his house. Satan has been defeated because the kingdom has made

its appearance in Jesus' ministry. Jesus is the stronger one because he is the holy one of God, the Son of God. Having already bound Satan in his great struggle with Satan in the wilderness (Matt 4:1-11), Jesus continues to bind him and plunder his house each time he heals or casts out demons.

Have you ever been "at a crossroads" where you had to choose for or against Jesus? What were the circumstances, and how did your choice affect your life or the lives of others?

"³⁰Whoever is not with me is against me, and whoever does not gather with me scatters."

Third, Jesus explains that this dramatic healing places us at a crossroads where we must decide what direction we will take. Will we join with Jesus in gathering others into the kingdom of God, or will we align ourselves with those who are scattering God's people because they refuse to embrace the kingdom of God? We are confronted with a decision for or against Jesus, for or against the kingdom.

The kingdom of God is more than an idea or theological concept. It is a dynamic reality that involves us in a great struggle between good and evil, God and Satan. To enter the kingdom is to enter the realm of God's rule that has *already begun* in Jesus Christ. To willfully refuse to recognize the kingdom is to remain under the rule and bondage of a cosmic power and a force opposed to all that is good.

Yes, the kingdom of God has come upon us. It is already here and present in the person and ministry of Jesus, continuing on in the ministry of the church, the community of believers. And so we are continually called to align ourselves with it, gathering others in, so that we may experience the healing and wholeness of God's reign.

> What are the signs in your life that the kingdom of God is "upon you"? How do you "gather others" into this saving reality?

Praying the Word / Sacred Reading

Psalm 23 is a gentle rendering of life in God's kingdom. To be a part of this kingdom is not to be a submissive vassal or even a dutiful citizen. Rather, to intentionally live within the reign of God is to be set free, to be loved and protected, to be—in the words of the psalmist—restored. Pray this psalm with a full awareness of the dignity and peace that come with experiencing the kingdom of God, where our King is not a tyrant but a shepherd.

The LORD is my shepherd;
    there is nothing I lack.
In green pastures he makes me lie down;
    to still waters he leads me;
    he restores my soul.

He guides me along right paths
    for the sake of his name.
Even though I walk through the valley of
        the shadow of death,
    I will fear no evil, for you are with me;
    your rod and your staff comfort me.

You set a table before me
    in front of my enemies;
You anoint my head with oil;
    my cup overflows.
Indeed, goodness and mercy will pursue me
    all the days of my life;
I will dwell in the house of the LORD
    for endless days. (Ps 23:1-6)

Living the Word

We may not think of ourselves as engaged in a "cosmic struggle between good and evil" as we await the fullness of God's kingdom, and yet we all join with Jesus in "pushing back the boundaries" of evil in our world.

How can you share in Jesus' healing ministry, which is a definitive sign of the in-breaking of God's kingdom?

Here are some ideas:

- *Visit someone in a hospital or nursing home.*

- *Visit a family member or fellow parishioner who rarely leaves their home due to illness or age.*

- *Spend time with a friend or family member struggling with mental illness.*

- *Renew your compassion for a loved one struggling with chronic pain or depression.*

- *Listen to those in your life who wish to share their pain with you. Listen without rushing and without distraction. Be a quiet, healing presence just by being with them.*

- *Commit to praying daily for someone in your life who struggles with physical or mental illness. Share your prayer commitment with him or her as a sign of your companionship in their time of illness.*

The Mystery of the Kingdom of God

Invite God to assist you in your prayer and study. Then read Matthew 13:24-35, the proclamation of the kingdom in parables.

Matthew 13:24-35

²⁴He proposed another parable to them. "The kingdom of heaven may be likened to a man who sowed good seed in his field. ²⁵While everyone was asleep his enemy came and sowed weeds all through the wheat, and then went off. ²⁶When the crop grew and bore fruit, the weeds appeared as well. ²⁷The slaves of the householder came to him and said, 'Master, did you not sow good seed in your field? Where have the weeds come from?' ²⁸He answered, 'An enemy has done this.' His slaves said to him, 'Do you want us to go and pull them up?' ²⁹He replied, 'No, if you pull up the weeds you might uproot the wheat along with them. ³⁰Let them grow together until harvest; then at harvest time I will say to the harvesters, "First collect the weeds and tie them in bundles for burning; but gather the wheat into my barn." ' "

[31]He proposed another parable to them. "The kingdom of heaven is like a mustard seed that a person took and sowed in a field. [32]It is the smallest of all the seeds, yet when full-grown it is the largest of plants. It becomes a large bush, and the 'birds of the sky come and dwell in its branches.'"

[33]He spoke to them another parable. "The kingdom of heaven is like yeast that a woman took and mixed with three measures of wheat flour until the whole batch was leavened."

[34]All these things Jesus spoke to the crowds in parables. He spoke to them only in parables, [35]to fulfill what had been said through the prophet:
"I will open my mouth in parables,
    I will announce what has lain hidden from
        the foundation [of the world]."

> *The information provided below in "Setting the Scene" will help you move from reflection to understanding by providing background information. Continue to use the questions in the margins to deepen your appreciation for how God's word addresses you.*

Setting the Scene

Our first Scripture passage taught us that the kingdom of God (understood as God's rule over creation and history) has made its appearance in Jesus' ministry. By curing the sick, casting out demons, and preaching the Good News of the kingdom, Jesus inaugurates the kingdom that he proclaims. But since the kingdom has not yet come with all of God's power and glory, it has a future dimension that we will consider in a number of parables.

Matthew 13 is the third of five great discourses that Jesus gives in the Gospel of Matthew, the other four being the Sermon on the Mount (chapters 5–7), the missionary discourse (chapter 10), the discourse on church life (chapter 18), and the discourse on Jesus' return at the end of the ages (chapters 24–25). In this third discourse, Jesus delivers a series of parables about the mystery of the kingdom of heaven (Matthew's way of referring to the kingdom of God).

Before we plunge into our text, however, it will be helpful to summarize the overall structure of Matthew 13 so that we understand how our parables (noted in italics) fit into the chapter as a whole:

13:1-3a	Setting: Jesus teaches the crowd from a boat on the sea
13:3b-9	Parable of the sower
13:10-17	Why Jesus teaches in parables
13:18-23	Jesus' explanation of the parable of the sower
13:24-30	*Parable of the weeds and the wheat*
13:31-32	*Parable of the mustard seed*
13:33	*Parable of the yeast*
13:34-35	*Why Jesus speaks in parables—to announce what was hidden*

13:36	Dismissal of the crowd and the disciples' question
13:37-43	Jesus' explanation of the parable of the weeds and the wheat
13:44	Parable of the buried treasure
13:45-46	Parable of the precious pearl
13:47-50	Parable of the net
13:51	Jesus' question and the disciples' response
13:52	Jesus' instruction to the disciples
13:53	Ending of the discourse

Notice that there are seven parables in Matthew 13, all of which deal with some aspect of the kingdom of God. We will reflect on three of them. Also note that Jesus explains the meaning of two of the parables. The disciples (who represent us) are in a privileged position because Jesus explains these parables to them, thereby showing them how to "decode" the other parables. We are also told that the parables reveal things "hidden from the foundation of the world" (the mystery of God's rule over our life) and that good disciples "understand" the mystery of the kingdom that Jesus reveals to them in these parables and live accordingly. Finally, at the end of this parable discourse in Matthew 13, Jesus declares that we, his disciples, should be "scribes" for the kingdom of heaven by making use of what is old (the Scriptures God has given us) and what is new (the kingdom of God).

Parables—or short stories that communicate a lesson—were among Jesus' favorite teaching tools. Why are stories an effective way to teach? Which of Jesus' parables comes to mind as your favorite?

*Matthew 13:24-35 will be considered
a few verses at a time to help digest
its meaning.*

Understanding the Scene Itself

²⁴He proposed another parable to them. "The kingdom of heaven may be likened to a man who sowed good seed in his field. ²⁵While everyone was asleep his enemy came and sowed weeds all through the wheat, and then went off. ²⁶When the crop grew and bore fruit, the weeds appeared as well. ²⁷The slaves of the householder came to him and said, 'Master, did you not sow good seed in your field? Where have the weeds come from?' ²⁸He answered, 'An enemy has done this.'"

This is the second parable that Jesus speaks to the crowd, the first being the parable of the sower, which Jesus has explained in private to his disciples. At the beginning of this parable, Jesus alerts us that there is a relationship between what he is about to say and the kingdom of heaven: "the kingdom of heaven *may be likened to . . . .*" Jesus will use the same expression at the beginning of the parable of the mustard seed (13:31) and the parable of the yeast (13:33).

The starting points for Jesus' parables are experiences and events that occur every day. In this case, Jesus speaks of the experience of a farmer who sows good seed only to discover that someone else has scattered weeds among the seed. A certain amount of time passes between the sowing of the seed and the appearance of the weeds. When the weeds make their appearance, the man's servants tell him what has happened. They are confused and want to know how this could have happened if their master sowed good seed. But the farmer understands what has occurred: his enemy has scattered weeds among the wheat to destroy his crop.

These first few verses of the parable already begin to prompt a number of questions: What does this story have to do with the kingdom of heaven? Who is the man who sows the good seed? What does the seed represent? Who are the man's servants? Who is the enemy, and why does he wish to destroy the farmer's crop?

Imagine yourself sitting on a hillside listening to Jesus teach. What is your impression of Jesus? What keeps you there? Why are you listening to him?

"His slaves said to him, 'Do you want us to go and pull them up?' ²⁹He replied, 'No, if you pull up the weeds you might uproot the wheat along with them. ³⁰Let them grow together until harvest; then at harvest time I will say to the harvesters, "First collect the weeds and tie them in bundles for burning; but gather the wheat into my barn." ' "

The immediate reaction of the slaves is to do what anyone who plants a garden would do: pull up the weeds so that the wheat can grow. But it is

precisely at this point that the parable takes an unexpected turn, and it is this unexpected turn that reveals something about the kingdom of heaven. Contrary to common wisdom, the farmer insists upon letting the wheat and the weeds grow together, promising that the harvesters will separate them at harvest time.

Like many of Jesus' parables, this is a story that resonates with our everyday experience, but it also surprises us. We understand that weeds make their annoying appearance in every garden, but why would anyone, aside from a lazy gardener, allow them to grow? There is something about this parable we must puzzle out.

Although the disciples should know how to interpret parables since Jesus has already shown them how to decode the parable of the sower (13:18-23), they do not (and perhaps we do not either!). And so Jesus must explain the parable to them and to us (see 13:36-43). Jesus is the Son of Man, the one who sows the seed. The good seeds that he sows are the children of the kingdom, and the field is the world. But then comes the enemy, the Evil One, who sows the weeds, which are his followers.

This is why at the present time, there is both good and bad in the world—and yes, in the church as well! This realization naturally leads us to ask (like the slaves in the parable): Wouldn't it be better if we could uproot all of those evil ones right now? Wouldn't it be better if we could have a "good world" now? Shouldn't we have a purified and reformed church right now, a church of people like ourselves?

That's the great temptation, isn't it? To clean house now! And to clean house according to our own standards. But Jesus understands that only God can judge the hearts of people. Only God knows the good and evil in our hearts. The final judgment, the moment of purification, will occur when the kingdom of heaven appears at the end of the ages. Then the harvesters, God's angels, will make known who the children of the Son of Man are (the wheat), and who the children of the Evil One are (the weeds).

The kingdom of God has come upon us in Jesus' ministry, but it has not yet appeared in all its glory, and so we live in a time of ambiguity, where good and evil exist side by side. It is an uncomfortable situation, and we want to take matters into our own hands. But sometimes the best thing we can do is to wait patiently as God's plan for the kingdom unfolds.

How does Jesus' parable of the weeds and the wheat challenge your way of understanding the church? Are you ever tempted to "weed out" a particular person or group, or have you ever experienced someone trying to "uproot" you?

[31]He proposed another parable to them. "The kingdom of heaven is like a mustard seed that a person took and sowed in a field. [32]It is the smallest of all the seeds, yet when full-grown it is the largest of plants. It becomes a large bush, and the 'birds of the sky come and dwell in its branches.' "

In the previous parable of the weeds and wheat Jesus taught us that we must live with ambiguity as we wait for the final appearance of the kingdom of heaven. In this parable of the mustard seed he teaches us that there is no comparison between the presence of the kingdom we experience now and the glory of the kingdom to come. Jesus says that the kingdom is like the tiniest of seeds. A seed appears so small and insignificant. But when the seed germinates and the plant is fully grown, we see the mysterious reality that was hidden in the seed. And so it is with the kingdom of God.

Reflect on an experience you have had of watching something grow—a plant, a child, even a building or a community. What changes, surprises, wonder, and amazement did you experience?

We experience something of God's kingdom in the Word we hear proclaimed in the liturgy, in the Eucharist in which we participate, in our communal life in Christ, in our personal prayer, and in the celebration of the sacraments. But the mysterious reality hidden behind these signs will only fully appear when the kingdom is revealed. The growth of the kingdom is hidden and mysterious. It is God's work in Christ with which we cooperate through the power of the Holy Spirit.

33He spoke to them another parable. "The kingdom of heaven is like yeast that a woman took and mixed with three measures of wheat flour until the whole batch was leavened."

The parable of the yeast is similar to the parable of the mustard seed and, on first hearing, we may ask if it is not merely repeating what we have already been taught. Like the previous parable, this is a parable that highlights the hidden and mysterious growth of God's rule over creation and history. But there is an interesting difference. In this parable, it is the yeast that brings about the growth. Without the yeast, the flour would not rise. What is this mysterious yeast that brings about such marvelous growth?

In Matthew 16:5-12, Jesus warns his disciples about the "yeast" or "leaven" of the Pharisees and Sadducees. At first, his disciples think that he is talking about ordinary bread. But when Jesus tells them he is not talking about bread but something else, the disciples understand that he is referring to "the *teaching* of the Pharisees and Sadducees," which stands in opposition to Jesus' teaching about the kingdom of heaven. The "yeast" that gives growth to the kingdom is Jesus' own teaching about the kingdom of heaven. At the present time, his teaching seems confined to a small, insignificant group of disciples, but his teaching is the yeast that will bring about the mysterious growth of the kingdom.

Something similar is still happening in the church today. We teach and preach, and it seems as if nothing is happening. We labor at the work of evangelization,

All three of these parables reveal that God's plans tend to unfold slowly—much more slowly than we might like. Reflect for a few moments on the beauty of slow things. Why do you think God works this way?

Do you ever have the feeling that "nothing is happening" in your family, your church community, or in your own ministry efforts? How do the parables of the mustard seed and the yeast help you to understand that something small and imperceptible may indeed be happening even when you cannot see it?

and it seems as if nothing is happening. But one day, through God's grace, our teaching, preaching, and evangelizing will come to fruition in the fullness of God's kingdom.

³⁴**All these things Jesus spoke to the crowds in parables. He spoke to them only in parables, ³⁵to fulfill what had been said through the prophet:**
"I will open my mouth in parables,
I will announce what has lain hidden from the foundation [of the world]."

Matthew concludes this chapter with his own commentary that summarizes the significance of Jesus' parables for us today. He notes that Jesus spoke in parables to fulfill what had been spoken by "the prophet." Although the quoted text comes from Psalm 78:3, Matthew understands it as a prophetic text since the whole of Scripture points prophetically to Christ. He is the one who opens his mouth in parables in order to reveal what was hidden from the foundation of the world—namely, the kingdom of God. This kingdom, understood as God's rule over our lives, is the great mystery that Jesus reveals through his life, death, and resurrection. It is the mystery of God's presence in our lives that will be revealed fully at the end of the age. Then we will understand how God was always present to us, even when we were not present to God. The kingdom has come; the fullness of the kingdom is yet to come.

God's kingdom—or God's presence—is always with us, even when we do not perceive it. How might we get better at recognizing God's kingdom in and among us?

But who is invited to the kingdom? That is the question to which we turn next.

Praying the Word / Sacred Reading

As you ponder the slow way that God's kingdom unfolds in the world and in our lives, offer this prayer slowly and thoughtfully. Or pray in your own words, asking God to reveal the fullness of the kingdom to you according to God's own plan and timing.

Lord Jesus, in your parables and your teachings,
you have taught us that God's ways are not
    our ways,
and that God's timing is not our timing.
When I want to speed God up,
grant me the patience to slow myself down.
When I want to weed out what I think is bad,
give me the wisdom to be still and wait.
When I want bread without yeast and plants
    before seeds,
gently remind me that the good things that
    God has in store take time.
And when I cannot perceive your kingdom,
show me where to look, so I may find you
among the weeds and the wheat until you
    come in glory.
Amen.

Living the Word

The image of the mustard seed transforming from a tiny seed into a large bush inhabited by the birds of the sky is a powerful one. This image can serve as a model for us in our own lives, relationships, and ministries.

- *Identify an area of your life where small changes are happening. Is God becoming increasingly present in those changes?*

- *Are your relationships prospering, stagnant, or falling apart? Identify a relationship that needs God's grace, and take steps to allow that grace to take root and bear fruit— reach out, forgive, work toward reconciliation, spend time together, offer help, express affection.*

- *Spend some time in prayer asking God how to use your gifts for the sake of others. What is some small thing you can do—just the size of a tiny mustard seed—that might benefit others the way a shady bush benefits a tired bird?*

The Universal Scope of the Kingdom of God

Invite God to assist you in your prayer and study. Then read the parable from Luke 14:15-24 that describes the kingdom in terms of a banquet and its guests.

Luke 14:15-24

[15]One of his fellow guests on hearing this said to him [Jesus], "Blessed is the one who will dine in the kingdom of God." [16]He replied to him, "A man gave a great dinner to which he invited many. [17]When the time for the dinner came, he dispatched his servant to say to those invited, 'Come, everything is now ready.' [18]But one by one, they all began to excuse themselves. The first said to him, 'I have purchased a field and must go to examine it; I ask you, consider me excused.' [19]And another said, 'I have purchased five yoke of oxen and am on my way to evaluate them; I ask you, consider me excused.'

[20]And another said, 'I have just married a woman, and therefore I cannot come.' [21]The servant went and reported this to his master. Then the master of the house in a rage commanded his servant, 'Go out quickly into the streets and alleys of the town and bring in here the poor and the crippled, the blind and the lame.' [22]The servant reported, 'Sir, your orders have been carried out and still there is room.' [23]The master then ordered the servant, 'Go out to the highways and hedgerows and make people come in that my home may be filled. [24]For, I tell you, none of those men who were invited will taste my dinner.'"

The information found in "Setting the Scene" provides a fuller context for appreciating the passage from Luke.

Setting the Scene

Thus far, we have seen that while the kingdom is already present in the ministry of Jesus, we are still waiting for its final coming in power and glory. When and how this will happen, we do not know. But we are confident that it *will* happen because of our trusting faith in Jesus Christ. In this section, we turn to another text (this one from the Gospel according to Luke) and to another question: *Who has been invited to the kingdom?* A chosen few? The righteous and the worthy? Or the many?

Our text is part of a larger section in Luke's gospel that recounts Jesus' final journey to Jerusalem (9:51–19:44). The material in this section can be likened to a catechism on discipleship in which Jesus instructs his followers how to live in the light of the kingdom that has made its appearance in his ministry.

Our text, which occurs in chapter 14, is especially enlightening in this regard. In the opening scene (14:1-6), Luke recounts how a prominent Pharisee invites Jesus to dine at his house where there is a man suffering from dropsy. It is the Sabbath, and everyone is wondering if Jesus will heal the sick man since healing might be construed as work that violates the Sabbath. Jesus asks the Mosaic Law scholars who are present if it is permitted to heal on the Sabbath. When they do not answer, he heals the man.

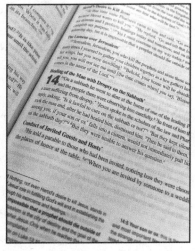

In the next scene (14:7-14), Jesus notices how the guests are choosing the first seats at the table. So he tells a parable that teaches them how to behave when they are invited to a banquet: take the lowest place rather than the place of honor, "[f]or everyone who exalts himself will be humbled, but the one who humbles himself will be exalted." Then Jesus instructs the Pharisee who invited him that when he gives a banquet he should invite those who will not be able to repay in kind: the poor, the crippled, the lame, and the blind. Then he will be repaid at the resurrection of the dead.

Since the resurrection of the dead is the moment when the kingdom of God will appear in glory, Jesus' teaching about taking the last place at banquets and inviting the poor clearly has something to do with the kingdom of God. Thus the first fourteen verses of this chapter serve as an introduction to our parable about the great banquet of God's kingdom.

> By considering the passage a few
> verses at a time, the text will
> become more meaningful.

Understanding the Scene Itself

[15]One of his fellow guests on hearing this said to him, "Blessed is the one who will dine in the kingdom of God."

If you have ever been at a dinner party where there has been an awkward silence because of what someone has said or done, then you understand this remark. Jesus has just healed a man on the Sabbath, and those present—especially the teachers of the Mosaic Law—are upset with him. In an attempt to break the awkward silence that follows, someone cries out, "Blessed is the one who will dine in the kingdom of God!" This is an appropriate remark in the sense that the meals that the Pharisees and Jesus celebrate are anticipations of the great banquet of God's king-

How do you imagine the "banquet" of God's kingdom?

dom. But what does this remark mean? What does it imply? Perhaps this man is suggesting that only a select few will dine in the kingdom of God—people like the Pharisees and experts in the Mosaic Law who diligently observe God's commandments. Surely they are the ones who will dine at the banquet of God's kingdom!

¹⁶He replied to him, "A man gave a great dinner to which he invited many. ¹⁷When the time for the dinner came, he dispatched his servant to say to those invited, 'Come, everything is now ready.' ¹⁸But one by one, they all began to excuse themselves. The first said to him, 'I have purchased a field and must go to examine it; I ask you, consider me excused.' ¹⁹And another said, 'I have purchased five yoke of oxen and am on my way to evaluate them; I ask you, consider me excused.' ²⁰And another said, 'I have just married a woman, and therefore I cannot come.' "

The remark intended to break the embarrassing silence becomes an occasion for Jesus to pronounce a second parable that echoes the teaching of his earlier parable about choosing the lowest place at banquets and inviting those who cannot reciprocate (14:7-14). In this parable, a man has prepared a grand banquet that has involved a great deal of time, effort, and expense. Now everything is ready. The guests have already accepted the invitation. They are well-to-do people of means, as will become apparent from their excuses. The man now sends his servant to tell the guests that everything is

Has God ever sent someone to invite you into his presence? Who was it, and what did the invitation sound like?

prepared: "Come quickly so that the food and drink will not spoil!" The host is not asking *if* they will come; that has already been settled. He is telling them that *now* is the time to come.

But, against all banquet etiquette, all of the invited guests—people of means and honor—excuse themselves. In doing so, they insult the host by the lameness of their excuses. The first two excuses have to do with business arrangements that have already been settled. Surely the man who purchased the field examined it before he bought it. Why must he examine it again? Surely the man who purchased the oxen evaluated them before he bought them. Why does he need to evaluate them again? And surely the man who has just been married knew he would be married when he accepted the invitation, so why is he refusing to come now?

But haven't we all made such lame excuses and told little white lies to get out of a social engagement at the last moment? "I am not feeling well." "I have a headache." "Something came up; I need to be somewhere else." Yes, we have all made such

excuses, and when we have, we are ashamed because we are breaking our word; we are no longer people of truth, honesty, and integrity. But there are also times when we excuse ourselves from more important matters that have to do with faith and trust in Jesus Christ:

"I would like to devote more time to prayer, but I don't have time." "I would like to devote more time to helping those in need, but I don't have time." Yes, there are always excuses.

"**²¹The servant went and reported this to his master. Then the master of the house in a rage commanded his servant, 'Go out quickly into the streets and alleys of the town and bring in here the poor and the crippled, the blind and the lame.'**"

The master is justly indignant at the lack of respect his guests have shown. He knows they have publicly shamed him. But he doesn't cancel the banquet. How can he? Everything is ready and prepared. And so he sends his servant into the less respectable parts of the city to invite the poor, the crippled, the blind, and the lame—the very people Jesus encourages us to invite when we give a dinner (14:13). These people don't "belong" at the banquet; there is no way they can reciprocate. More than that, they would never have imagined that this man of means would invite them. They don't belong here (nor do we), but they (and we) are invited.

"**²²The servant reported, 'Sir, your orders have been carried out and still there is room.' ²³The master then ordered the servant, 'Go out to the highways and hedgerows and make people come in that my home may be filled. ²⁴For, I tell you, none of those men who were invited will taste my dinner.'**"

> The invited guests have other priorities that cause them to miss out on the great dinner prepared for them. Is there anything in your life that is distracting you from entering more fully into God's kingdom?

> God loves us in a generous way that we cannot fully reciprocate. We strive to love others in the same way. Who are those in your life who cannot reciprocate? Who is Jesus asking you to love generously?

After the servant has carried out his master's orders, he reports that there is still room at the banquet. It is now apparent how truly great the banquet is that the man has prepared! It is not for a few guests; it is for a great multitude of people. And so the master sends his servant out a second time. This time, the servant is to go outside the city and invite whomever he finds so that the banquet hall will be filled. It does not matter who the people are; they are invited. The master is no longer concerned about the social status of his guests. His primary concern is to fill the banquet hall until it is overflowing with guests of every sort. And fill it he will—with everyone except those who were originally invited!

What a great reversal! The original banquet was for the elite and the privileged—for those who could return the favor. The final banquet is for everybody—especially the poor and the down-trodden, who never expected to be invited and who will never be able to repay their host. Everyone is welcome. No one is excluded, unless they exclude themselves by refusing the invitation.

The occasion for this parable is a simple remark intended to break the tension in the place where Jesus was dining with a Pharisee. That remark implied that only a few blessed ones (like the speaker) expected to be invited to the banquet of God's kingdom. With this parable, Jesus shatters this theology of privilege. He shatters *our* theology of privilege. The kingdom of God is not for the few but for the many: the poor, the crippled, the lame, and the blind. Are we not all poor when we stand before God? Are we not all crippled and lame on account of our sinfulness? Are we not all blind to the generosity and goodness of God? Yes, the kingdom of God is always bringing about a reversal of fortunes so that the last will be first, and the first will be last (see Luke 1:46-55; 6:20-26).

We may all hold to some "theology of privilege" that favors certain people and excludes certain others. How does this parable challenge you personally?

But, we might ask, isn't this unfair? If people are invited so indiscriminately into the kingdom of God, it would seem there is nothing they need to do but "show up"! And yes, we do need to "show up"—but first, we must *accept the invitation* by receiving God's grace into our lives. This interior act of accepting God's invitation to be present in our lives is what allows us to receive God's extravagant grace, the grace of God's kingdom that changes and transforms us.

> *The kingdom of God is always bringing about a reversal of fortunes so that the last will be first, and the first will be last.*

This parable touches on the relationship between grace (what God does in us) and free will (what we choose to do). How do grace and your own free will work together? Are they ever opposed?

We know that Jesus does not actually want us to "hate" our families or our own lives. But what is the effect of the strong language Jesus uses here (14:26)? Why must following Jesus be our first priority?

Put another way, we have not been invited to the banquet of the kingdom because we are good. We have been invited because God is generous beyond all measure. But when we *accept* God's invitation, God's grace touches our lives and transforms us into the holiness of Christ so that we can live the life of discipleship. This is why we "belong" in God's kingdom—not because of what we have done, but because of what God does in us.

It is not by chance that in the next episode Jesus teaches those who follow him the demands of discipleship (14:25-35). A great crowd is accompanying Jesus, expecting the appearance of the kingdom of God. As the crowd follows, Jesus turns and warns, "If anyone comes to me without hating his father and mother, wife and children brothers and sisters, and even his own life, he cannot be my disciple" (14:26). The unmerited grace of the kingdom of God and the demands of discipleship are two sides of a coin. From start to finish, everything is grace, and it is this unmerited grace that allows us to live as faithful disciples.

As we look back on our gospel texts, we can see the scope of Jesus' teaching about the kingdom of God. The kingdom of God is God's rule over our lives. It has already made its appearance in Jesus' life, death, and resurrection. It is here. We experience it daily. But the fullness of the kingdom will only arrive in God's way, in God's time, at the end of the ages when we share in the resurrection of the dead. And finally, this kingdom—God's rule over our lives in Christ—

is breathtaking in scope. It includes all who accept the invitation. Only those who exclude themselves will not sit at the banquet of the kingdom of God. For all is grace—unmerited grace—lived in faithful discipleship.

What new perspective do you have on the kingdom of God? How will you share it with others?

Praying the Word / Sacred Reading

Jesus has invited us to the feast, to rejoice in his presence. Will we make excuses? Or will we attend the feast? Meditate on this invitation of Jesus from the book of Revelation. Respond to Jesus in prayer.

> "Behold, I stand at the door and knock. If anyone hears my voice and opens the door, [then] I will enter his house and dine with him, and he with me." (Rev 3:20)

Lord Jesus, may we hear you when you knock. Give us the wisdom, the focus, and the discipline to respond, to answer the door, to invite you into our lives. May we never leave you on the outside.

Help us to see all of our excuses for what they really are—obstacles between ourselves and you, lame substitutes for the kingdom of God, shadows and imitations of the beauty you offer.

Enter our homes and dine with us. Enter our hearts and be with us.

Living the Word

As the parable of the great dinner illustrates, Jesus was known for bold and surprising inclusiveness. This is a challenge for all of us!

- How does the parable of the great dinner challenge you to be more inclusive as a disciple of Jesus? Can you invite someone into your life that you may have excluded in the past? How can you provide this person (or this group of people) with a great feast of love, service, and friendship?

- This parable also challenges our parish communities. Identify several ways that your parish can be more inviting and welcoming. If you feel so called, invest yourself in this work of discipleship.